Recipes to make your own gifts!

Use these recipes to delight your friends and family. Each recipe includes gift tags for your convenience – just cut them out and personalize. After personalizing your tag, attach it to the bottle using raffia, ribbon, twine or yarn.

Use a variety of different bottle sizes and shapes according to your tastes. Depending on the size of the recipe and bottles you use, you may be able to fill 1, 2 or even 3 bottles. Decorative bottles can be found at craft or import stores. (Or keep your eyes open at garage sales and flea markets!)

Printed in the United States of America
by G&R Publishing Co.

Distributed By:

507 Industrial Street
Waverly, IA 50677

ISBN 1-56383-180-5
Item # 3440

Bigger Than Texas Hot Sauce

Makes 1 1/2 cups

1/2 C. chopped green jalapeno peppers
1/2 C. chopped roasted red peppers
1/2 C. chopped garlic
2 T. rice wine vinegar
Salt to taste

Remove seeds from chopped peppers. In a blender or food processor, combine chopped jalapeno peppers, chopped roasted red peppers, chopped garlic and vinegar. Puree mixture until smooth. Add salt to taste. Using a funnel, transfer sauce to a decorative sealable bottle. Cover bottle tightly and store in refrigerator.

Attach a gift tag with directions on how to serve sauce.

Gift Tag Directions:

Bigger Than Texas Hot Sauce

Use Bigger Than Texas Hot Sauce in recipes calling for hot sauce or serve with sandwiches, burgers, chips or anything that needs a kick! Store in refrigerator.

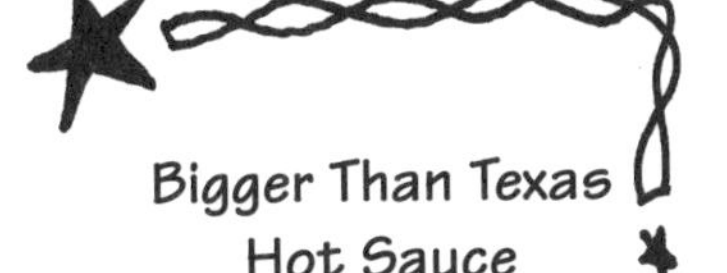

Bigger Than Texas Hot Sauce

Use Bigger Than Texas Hot Sauce in recipes calling for hot sauce or serve with sandwiches, burgers, chips or anything that needs a kick! Store in refrigerator.

Bigger Than Texas Hot Sauce

Use Bigger Than Texas Hot Sauce in recipes calling for hot sauce or serve with sandwiches, burgers, chips or anything that needs a kick! Store in refrigerator.

Bigger Than Texas Hot Sauce

Use Bigger Than Texas Hot Sauce in recipes calling for hot sauce or serve with sandwiches, burgers, chips or anything that needs a kick! Store in refrigerator.

Bigger Than Texas Hot Sauce

Use Bigger Than Texas Hot Sauce in recipes calling for hot sauce or serve with sandwiches, burgers, chips or anything that needs a kick! Store in refrigerator.

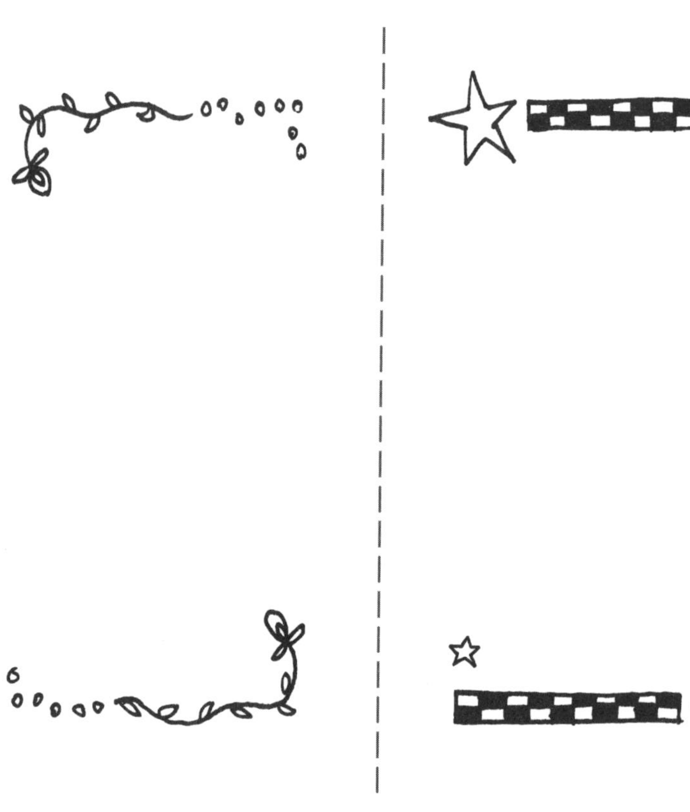

Red Glare BBQ Sauce

Makes 1 quart

2 (12 oz.) bottles chili sauce
2 cloves garlic, minced
1/3 C. ketchup
1/3 C. cider vinegar
1/3 C. brown sugar
3 T. Worcestershire sauce
3 T. sherry cooking wine
2 T. chili powder
2 tsp. ground cumin
1 tsp. crushed red pepper

In a medium saucepan over medium high heat, combine chili sauce, minced garlic, ketchup, cider vinegar, brown sugar, Worcestershire sauce, sherry, chili powder, ground cumin and crushed red pepper. Bring mixture to a boil. Reduce heat and simmer for 20 minutes, stirring occasionally, until sauce thickens. Using a funnel, transfer sauce to a decorative sealable bottle. Cover bottle tightly and store in refrigerator.

Attach a gift tag with directions on how to serve sauce.

Gift Tag Directions:

Red Glare BBQ Sauce

Use Red Glare BBQ Sauce as a dipping sauce for meat, smothered over steaks, pork or chicken or in recipes calling for barbeque sauce. Store in refrigerator.

Red Glare BBQ Sauce

Use Red Glare BBQ Sauce as a dipping sauce for meat, smothered over steaks, pork or chicken or in recipes calling for barbeque sauce. Store in refrigerator.

Red Glare BBQ Sauce

Use Red Glare BBQ Sauce as a dipping sauce for meat, smothered over steaks, pork or chicken or in recipes calling for barbeque sauce. Store in refrigerator.

Red Glare BBQ Sauce

Use Red Glare BBQ Sauce as a dipping sauce for meat, smothered over steaks, pork or chicken or in recipes calling for barbeque sauce. Store in refrigerator.

Red Glare BBQ Sauce

Use Red Glare BBQ Sauce as a dipping sauce for meat, smothered over steaks, pork or chicken or in recipes calling for barbeque sauce. Store in refrigerator.

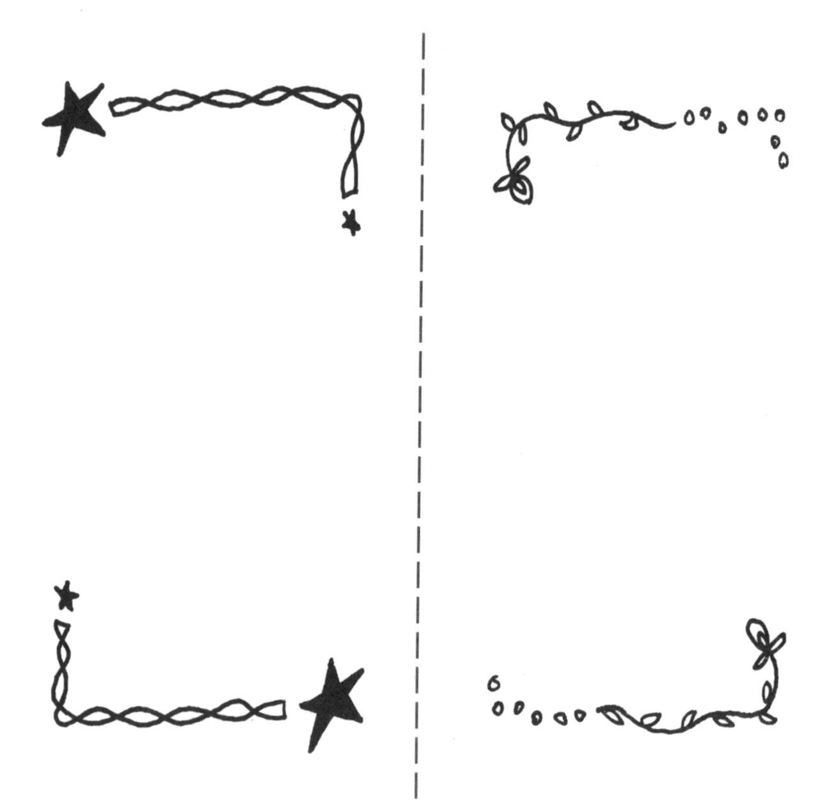

Chocolate Peppermint Sauce

Makes 1 1/2 cups

20 peppermint hard candies, unwrapped
1 C. milk
2 T. chocolate syrup
1/4 C. instant chocolate pudding mix
1/8 tsp. peppermint extract
Pinch of salt

In a double boiler over low medium heat, combine peppermint candies, milk, chocolate syrup, chocolate pudding mix, peppermint extract and salt. Stir over simmering water until melted. Mix until well blended. Using a funnel, transfer sauce to a decorative sealable bottle. Cover bottle tightly and store in refrigerator up to 10 days.

Attach a gift tag with directions on how to serve sauce.

Gift Tag Directions:

Chocolate Peppermint Sauce

Heat Chocolate Peppermint Sauce in microwave for 1 to 1 1/2 minutes. Use sauce as a topping for ice cream or drizzled over chocolate brownies. Store in refrigerator and discard after 10 days.

Chocolate Peppermint Sauce

Heat Chocolate Peppermint Sauce in microwave for 1 to 1 1/2 minutes. Use sauce as a topping for ice cream or drizzled over chocolate brownies. Store in refrigerator and discard after 10 days.

Chocolate Peppermint Sauce

Heat Chocolate Peppermint Sauce in microwave for 1 to 1 1/2 minutes. Use sauce as a topping for ice cream or drizzled over chocolate brownies. Store in refrigerator and discard after 10 days.

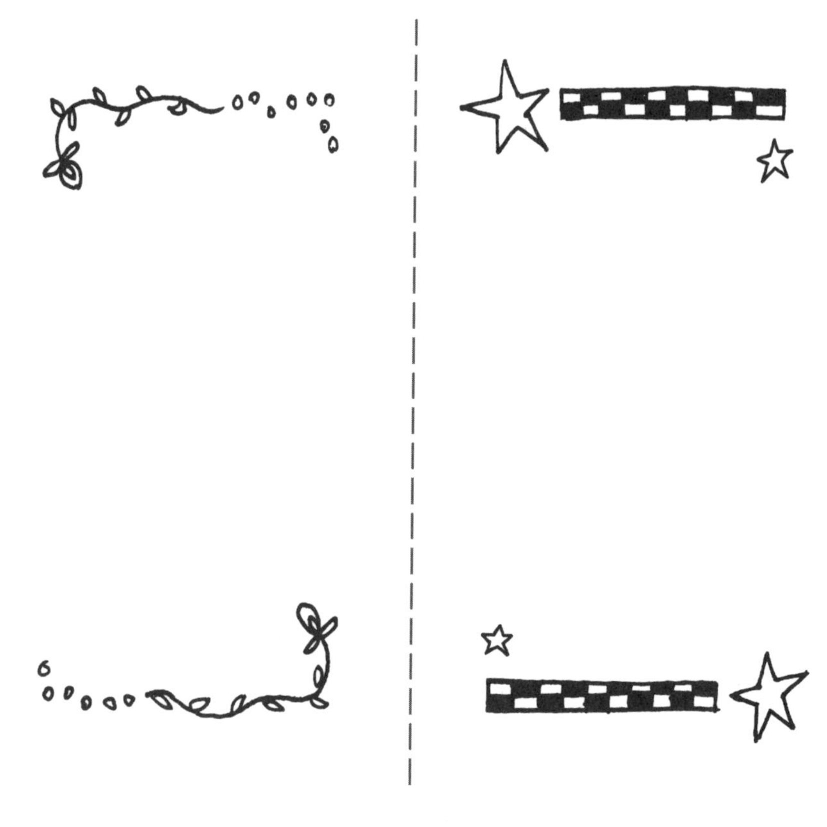

Chocolate Peppermint Sauce

Heat Chocolate Peppermint Sauce in microwave for 1 to 1 1/2 minutes. Use sauce as a topping for ice cream or drizzled over chocolate brownies. Store in refrigerator and discard after 10 days.

Chocolate Peppermint Sauce

Heat Chocolate Peppermint Sauce in microwave for 1 to 1 1/2 minutes. Use sauce as a topping for ice cream or drizzled over chocolate brownies. Store in refrigerator and discard after 10 days.

Jalapeno Hot Sauce

Makes 1 quart

1 1/2 lbs. green jalapeno peppers
5 C. vinegar
3 T. salt
1 C. water

Cut jalapeno peppers crosswise into slices. Remove most of the stems and seeds. In a large saucepan over medium high heat, combine sliced jalapeno peppers, vinegar, salt and water. Bring mixture to a boil. Reduce heat and let simmer for 20 to 30 minutes. Remove from heat and let sit until mixture reaches room temperature. Drain jalapeno slices from mixture, reserving 1 cup liquid. In a blender or food processor, puree drained jalapeno slices and 1 cup reserved liquid until smooth. Return puree to saucepan over medium high heat and bring to a boil. Reduce heat and let simmer for 10 to 20 minutes, until sauce reaches desired thickness. Using a funnel, transfer sauce to a decorative sealable bottle. Cover bottle tightly and store in refrigerator.

Attach a gift tag with directions on how to serve sauce.

Gift Tag Directions:

Jalapeno Hot Sauce

Use Jalapeno Hot Sauce in recipes calling for hot sauce or serve with eggs, tacos, burritos, chicken, pork, fish or anything that needs a kick! Store in refrigerator.

Jalapeno Hot Sauce

Use Jalapeno Hot Sauce in recipes calling for hot sauce or serve with eggs, tacos, burritos, chicken, pork, fish or anything that needs a kick! Store in refrigerator.

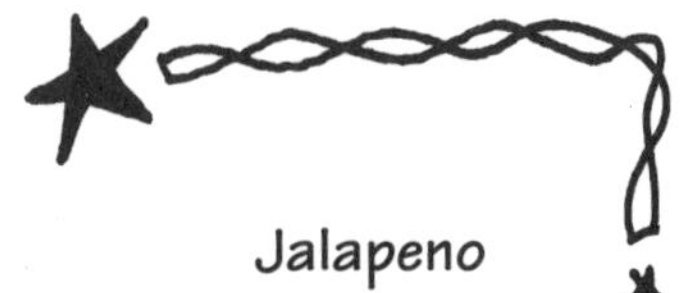

Jalapeno Hot Sauce

Use Jalapeno Hot Sauce in recipes calling for hot sauce or serve with eggs, tacos, burritos, chicken, pork, fish or anything that needs a kick! Store in refrigerator.

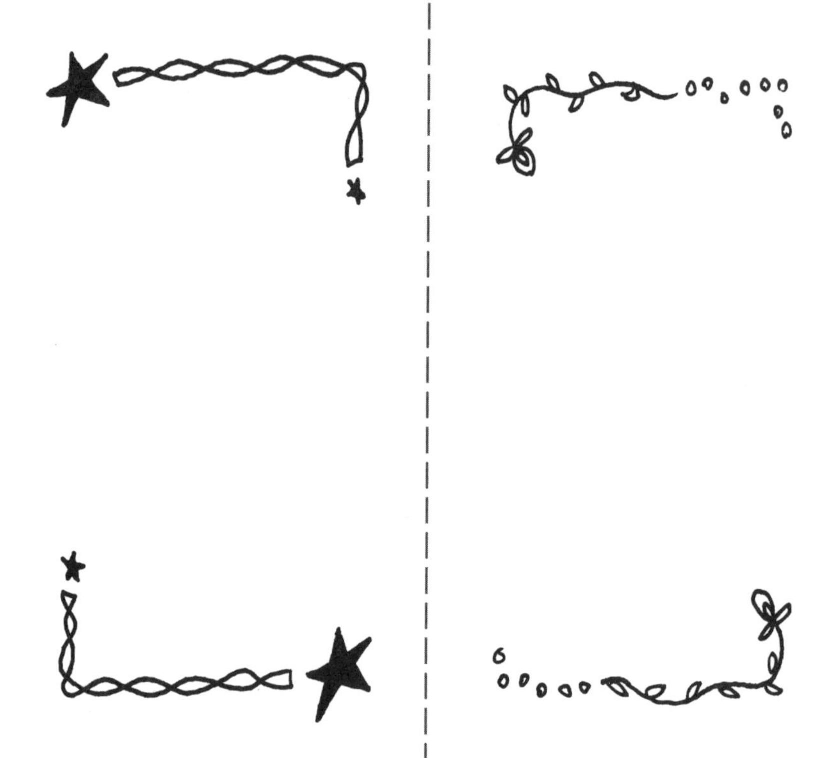

Jalapeno Hot Sauce

Use Jalapeno Hot Sauce in recipes calling for hot sauce or serve with eggs, tacos, burritos, chicken, pork, fish or anything that needs a kick! Store in refrigerator.

Jalapeno Hot Sauce

Use Jalapeno Hot Sauce in recipes calling for hot sauce or serve with eggs, tacos, burritos, chicken, pork, fish or anything that needs a kick! Store in refrigerator.

Praline Sundae Sauce

Makes 2 1/2 cups

1/4 C. butter or margarine
1 1/4 C. brown sugar
16 large marshmallows
2 T. light corn syrup
Pinch of salt
1 C. evaporated milk
1/2 C. chopped pecans, toasted*
1 tsp. vanilla

In a large saucepan, melt butter over medium heat. Add brown sugar, marshmallows, light corn syrup and salt. Cook, stirring constantly, over low heat until marshmallows are melted and mixture comes to a boil. Let boil for 1 minute and remove from heat. Let cool for 3 minutes. Stir in evaporated milk, toasted pecans and vanilla. Mix until well blended. Using a funnel, transfer sauce to a decorative sealable bottle. Cover bottle tightly and store in refrigerator.

* To toast, place chopped pecans in a single layer on a baking sheet. Bake at 350* for approximately 10 minutes or until pecans are golden brown.

Attach a gift tag with directions on how to serve sauce.

Gift Tag Directions:

Praline Sundae Sauce

Heat Praline Sundae Sauce in microwave for 1 to 1 1/2 minutes or warm over low heat before serving. Use sauce as a topping for ice cream or drizzled over brownies or cake. Store in refrigerator.

Praline Sundae Sauce

Heat Praline Sundae Sauce in microwave for 1 to 1 1/2 minutes or warm over low heat before serving. Use sauce as a topping for ice cream or drizzled over brownies or cake. Store in refrigerator.

Praline Sundae Sauce

Heat Praline Sundae Sauce in microwave for 1 to 1 1/2 minutes or warm over low heat before serving. Use sauce as a topping for ice cream or drizzled over brownies or cake. Store in refrigerator.

Praline Sundae Sauce

Heat Praline Sundae Sauce in microwave for 1 to 1 1/2 minutes or warm over low heat before serving. Use sauce as a topping for ice cream or drizzled over brownies or cake. Store in refrigerator.

Praline Sundae Sauce

Heat Praline Sundae Sauce in microwave for 1 to 1 1/2 minutes or warm over low heat before serving. Use sauce as a topping for ice cream or drizzled over brownies or cake. Store in refrigerator.

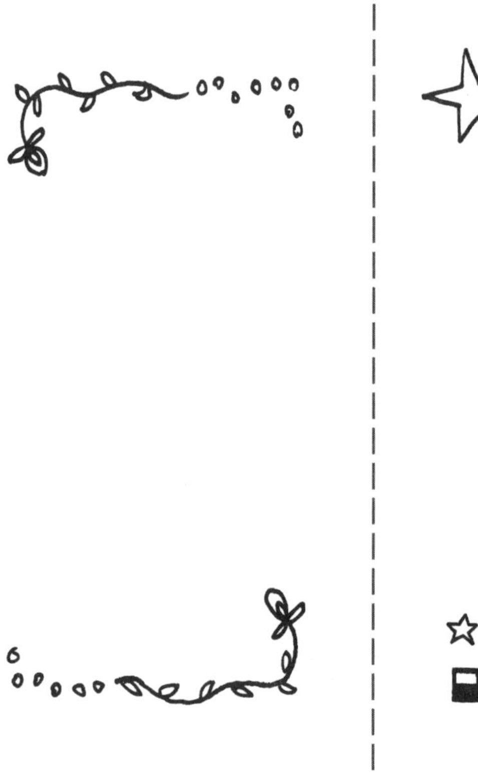

Smokey BBQ Sauce

Makes 1 quart

1 (18 oz.) bottle barbeque sauce
5 oz. salsa
1/2 C. soy sauce
3/4 C. brown sugar
1 tsp. ground ginger
1 T. minced garlic
1 T. pepper
Salt to taste

In a large bowl, combine barbeque sauce, salsa, soy sauce, brown sugar, ginger, minced garlic and pepper. Mix until well blended. Add salt to taste. Using a funnel, transfer sauce to a decorative sealable bottle. Cover bottle tightly and store in refrigerator.

Attach a gift tag with directions on how to serve sauce.

Gift Tag Directions:

Smokey BBQ Sauce

Use Smokey BBQ Sauce as a marinade for smoked meat, smothered over grilled steaks, pork or chicken or in recipes calling for barbeque sauce. Store in refrigerator.

Smokey BBQ Sauce

Use Smokey BBQ Sauce as a marinade for smoked meat, smothered over grilled steaks, pork or chicken or in recipes calling for barbeque sauce. Store in refrigerator.

Smokey BBQ Sauce

Use Smokey BBQ Sauce as a marinade for smoked meat, smothered over grilled steaks, pork or chicken or in recipes calling for barbeque sauce. Store in refrigerator.

Smokey BBQ Sauce

Use Smokey BBQ Sauce as a marinade for smoked meat, smothered over grilled steaks, pork or chicken or in recipes calling for barbeque sauce. Store in refrigerator.

Smokey BBQ Sauce

Use Smokey BBQ Sauce as a marinade for smoked meat, smothered over grilled steaks, pork or chicken or in recipes calling for barbeque sauce. Store in refrigerator.

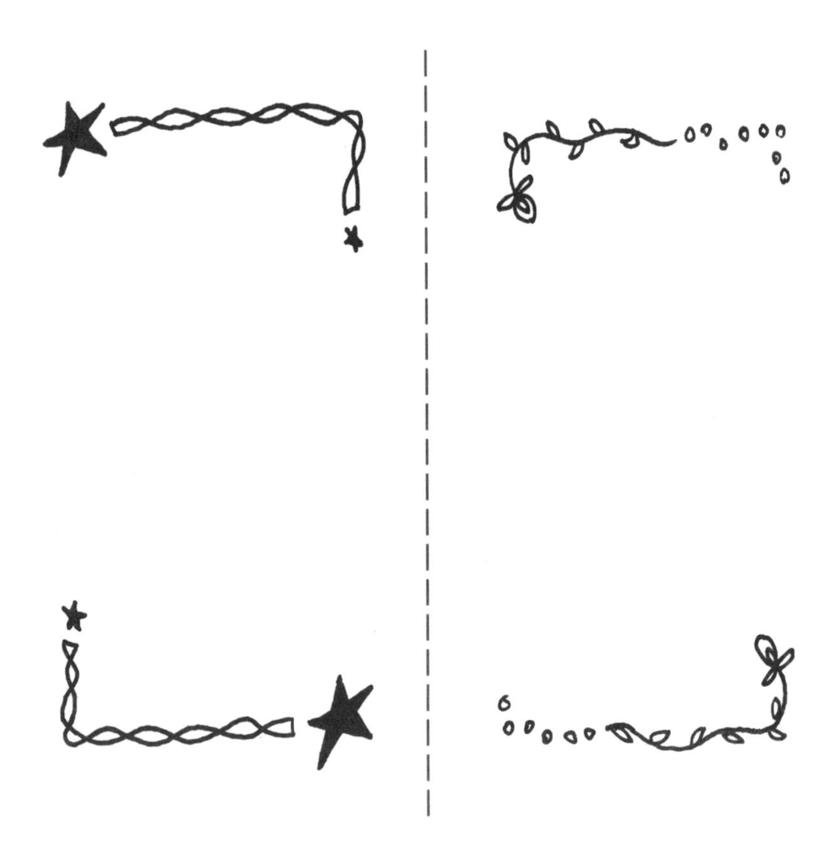

Peanut Butter Dessert Sauce

Make 2 1/2 cups

1 C. brown sugar
1/2 C. light corn syrup
3 T. butter or margarine
Pinch of salt
1 C. creamy peanut butter
1/2 C. evaporated milk

In a medium microwave-safe bowl, combine brown sugar, light corn syrup, butter and salt. Cover bowl and microwave on high for 3 minutes, removing to stir after every minute, until mixture boils. Add peanut butter and stir until smooth. Stir in evaporated milk. Using a funnel, transfer sauce to a decorative sealable bottle. Cover bottle tightly and store in refrigerator.

Attach a gift tag with directions on how to serve sauce.

Gift Tag Directions:

Peanut Butter Dessert Sauce

Heat Peanut Butter Dessert Sauce in microwave for 1 to 1 1/2 minutes or warm over low heat before serving. Use sauce as a topping for ice cream, drizzled over brownies or cake or as a dipping sauce for apple slices. Store in refrigerator.

Peanut Butter Dessert Sauce

Heat Peanut Butter Dessert Sauce in microwave for 1 to 1 1/2 minutes or warm over low heat before serving. Use sauce as a topping for ice cream, drizzled over brownies or cake or as a dipping sauce for apple slices. Store in refrigerator.

Peanut Butter Dessert Sauce

Heat Peanut Butter Dessert Sauce in microwave for 1 to 1 1/2 minutes or warm over low heat before serving. Use sauce as a topping for ice cream, drizzled over brownies or cake or as a dipping sauce for apple slices. Store in refrigerator.

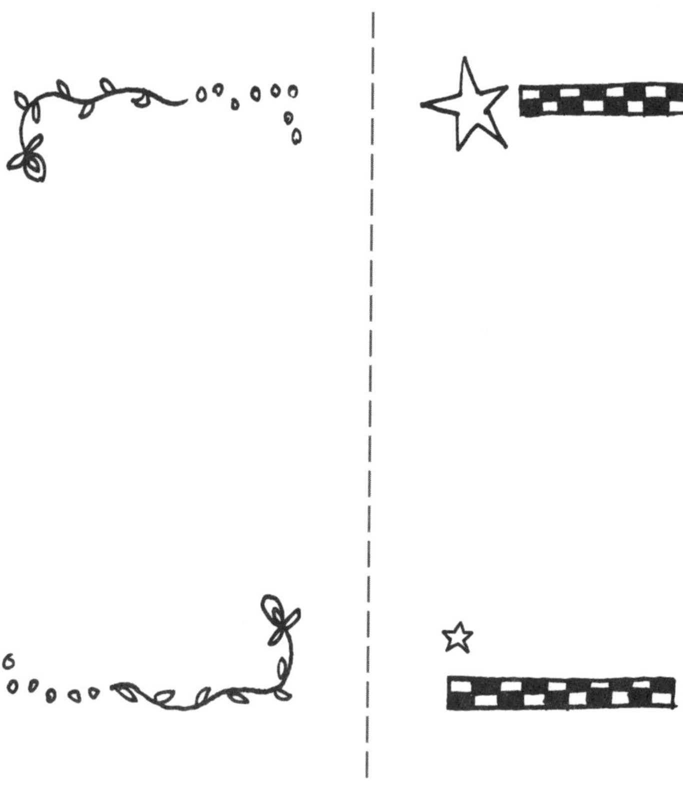

Peanut Butter Dessert Sauce

Heat Peanut Butter Dessert Sauce in microwave for 1 to 1 1/2 minutes or warm over low heat before serving. Use sauce as a topping for ice cream, drizzled over brownies or cake or as a dipping sauce for apple slices. Store in refrigerator.

Peanut Butter Dessert Sauce

Heat Peanut Butter Dessert Sauce in microwave for 1 to 1 1/2 minutes or warm over low heat before serving. Use sauce as a topping for ice cream, drizzled over brownies or cake or as a dipping sauce for apple slices. Store in refrigerator.

Apple BBQ Sauce

Makes 1 quart

1 C. ketchup
3/4 tsp. white pepper
1/2 C. apple juice concentrate
1/3 C. peeled diced apples
1/4 C. apple cider vinegar
1/4 C. diced onions
1/4 C. soy sauce
2 tsp. diced green peppers
3/4 tsp. garlic powder

In a large pot over medium heat, combine ketchup, white pepper, apple juice concentrate, diced apples, vinegar, diced onions, soy sauce, diced green peppers and garlic powder. Bring to a boil. Reduce heat and let simmer for 15 minutes. If smooth sauce is preferred, transfer to a blender or food processor and puree. Using a funnel, transfer sauce to a decorative sealable bottle. Cover bottle tightly and store in refrigerator.

Attach a gift tag with directions on how to serve sauce.

Gift Tag Directions:

Apple BBQ Sauce

Use Apple BBQ Sauce as a dipping sauce for meat, smothered over steaks, pork or chicken or in recipes calling for barbeque sauce. Store in refrigerator.

Apple BBQ Sauce

Use Apple BBQ Sauce as a dipping sauce for meat, smothered over steaks, pork or chicken or in recipes calling for barbeque sauce. Store in refrigerator.

Apple BBQ Sauce

Use Apple BBQ Sauce as a dipping sauce for meat, smothered over steaks, pork or chicken or in recipes calling for barbeque sauce. Store in refrigerator.

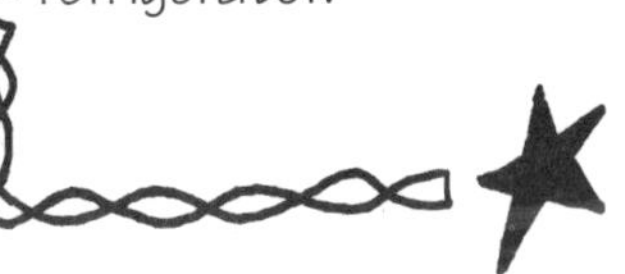

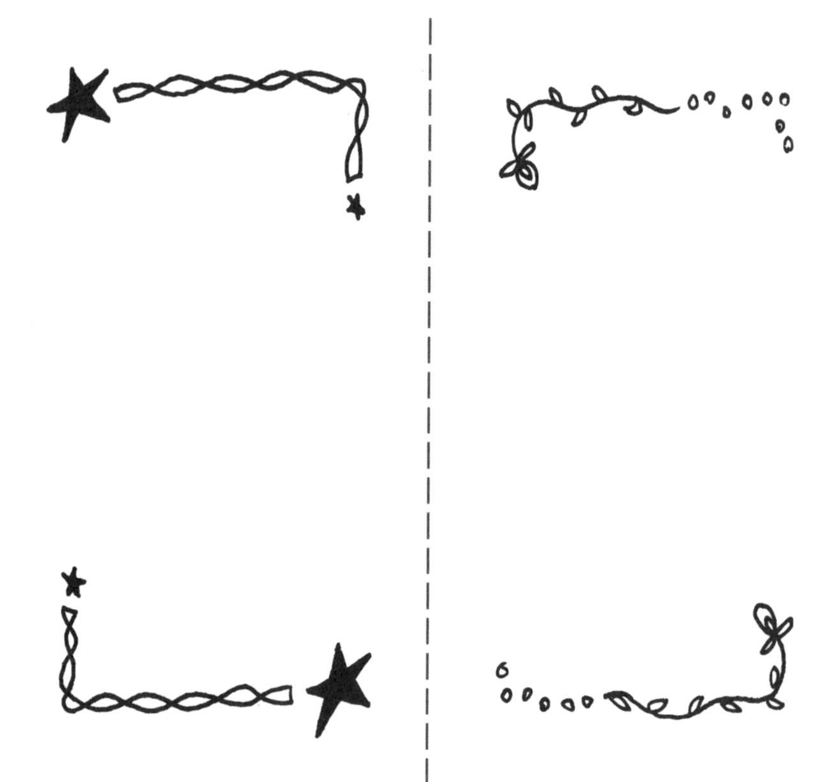

Apple BBQ Sauce

Use Apple BBQ Sauce as a dipping sauce for meat, smothered over steaks, pork or chicken or in recipes calling for barbeque sauce. Store in refrigerator.

Apple BBQ Sauce

Use Apple BBQ Sauce as a dipping sauce for meat, smothered over steaks, pork or chicken or in recipes calling for barbeque sauce. Store in refrigerator.

Tomatillo Chipotle Sauce

Makes 1 quart

12 large tomatillos
2 cloves garlic, minced
3 T. olive oil, divided
1/2 onion, finely chopped
4 canned chipotle chilies in adobo sauce
2 tsp. adobo sauce
1 bunch cilantro, leaves only
1 tsp. salt
Juice of 1 lime

Husk and wash tomatillos under hot water. In a heavy skillet over medium high heat, cook tomatillos for 10 to 15 minutes, stirring occasionally, until soft and blackened. Be careful not to let tomatillos dry out. Add minced garlic to skillet and cook until softened. In a medium saucepan, heat 1 tablespoon olive oil and sauté onions until softened and browned. In a blender or food processor, combine roasted tomatillos, roasted garlic, remaining 2 tablespoons olive oil, cooked onions, chipotle chilies, adobo sauce, cilantro leaves and salt. Puree mixture until smooth, adding water if necessary. Add lime juice and blend for a few additional seconds. Using a funnel, transfer sauce to a decorative sealable bottle. Cover bottle tightly and store in refrigerator up to 10 days.

Attach a gift tag with directions on how to serve sauce.

Gift Tag Directions:

Tomatillo Chipotle Sauce

Serve Tomatillo Chipotle Sauce hot or cold. Excellent as a chip dip. If desired, serve with roasted pork, grilled fish, chicken, enchiladas, tacos or burritos. Store in refrigerator and discard after 10 days.

Tomatillo Chipotle Sauce

Serve Tomatillo Chipotle Sauce hot or cold. Excellent as a chip dip. If desired, serve with roasted pork, grilled fish, chicken, enchiladas, tacos or burritos. Store in refrigerator and discard after 10 days.

Tomatillo Chipotle Sauce

Serve Tomatillo Chipotle Sauce hot or cold. Excellent as a chip dip. If desired, serve with roasted pork, grilled fish, chicken, enchiladas, tacos or burritos. Store in refrigerator and discard after 10 days.

Tomatillo Chipotle Sauce

Serve Tomatillo Chipotle Sauce hot or cold. Excellent as a chip dip. If desired, serve with roasted pork, grilled fish, chicken, enchiladas, tacos or burritos. Store in refrigerator and discard after 10 days.

Tomatillo Chipotle Sauce

Serve Tomatillo Chipotle Sauce hot or cold. Excellent as a chip dip. If desired, serve with roasted pork, grilled fish, chicken, enchiladas, tacos or burritos. Store in refrigerator and discard after 10 days.

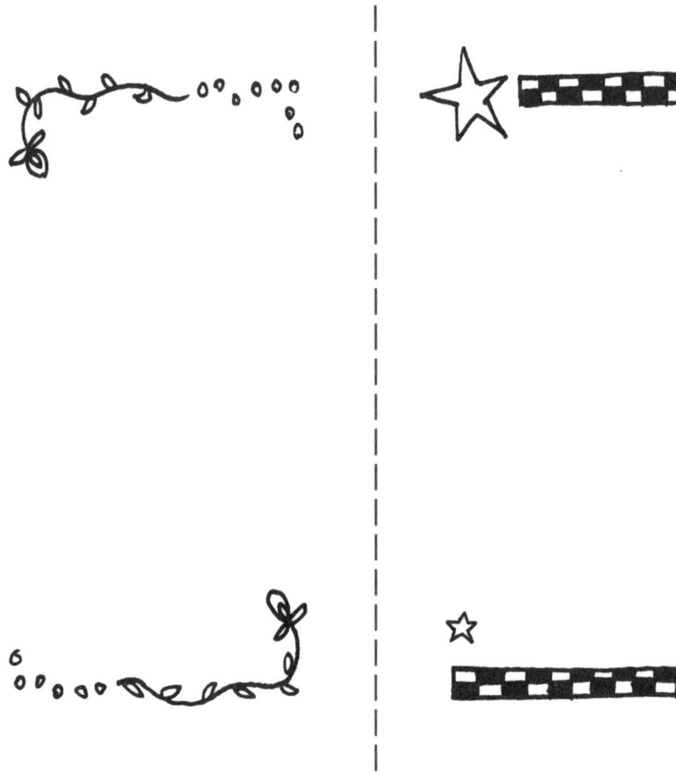

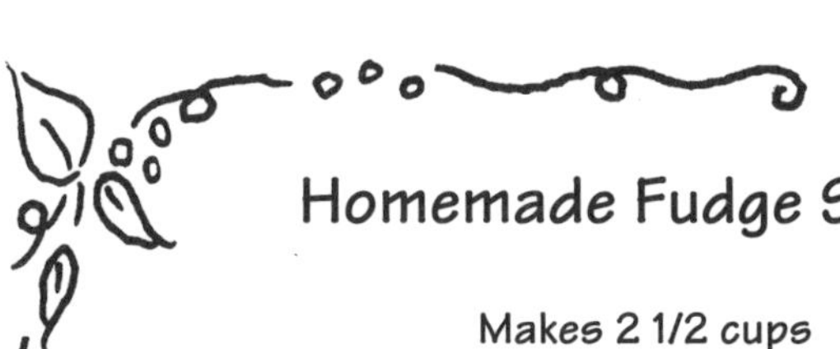

Homemade Fudge Sauce

Makes 2 1/2 cups

1 C. butter
1/3 C. cocoa powder
3 C. sugar
1 (12 oz.) can evaporated milk
1 tsp. vanilla

In a medium saucepan over medium heat, combine butter, cocoa powder, sugar and evaporated milk. Bring mixture to a boil, stirring constantly. Let boil for 7 minutes and remove from heat. Stir in vanilla. Carefully pour hot mixture into a blender. Blend for 2 to 3 minutes. Using a funnel, transfer sauce to a decorative sealable bottle. Cover bottle tightly and store in refrigerator up to 1 week.

Attach a gift tag with directions on how to serve sauce.

Gift Tag Directions:

Homemade Fudge Sauce

Warm Homemade Fudge Sauce over low heat before serving. Use sauce as a topping for ice cream or drizzled over chocolate brownies or cake. Store in refrigerator and discard after 1 week.

Homemade Fudge Sauce

Warm Homemade Fudge Sauce over low heat before serving. Use sauce as a topping for ice cream or drizzled over chocolate brownies or cake. Store in refrigerator and discard after 1 week.

Homemade Fudge Sauce

Warm Homemade Fudge Sauce over low heat before serving. Use sauce as a topping for ice cream or drizzled over chocolate brownies or cake. Store in refrigerator and discard after 1 week.

Homemade Fudge Sauce

Warm Homemade Fudge Sauce over low heat before serving. Use sauce as a topping for ice cream or drizzled over chocolate brownies or cake. Store in refrigerator and discard after 1 week.

Homemade Fudge Sauce

Warm Homemade Fudge Sauce over low heat before serving. Use sauce as a topping for ice cream or drizzled over chocolate brownies or cake. Store in refrigerator and discard after 1 week.

Tinglin' Tongue Hot Sauce

Makes 1 1/2 quarts

- 64 oz. canned chopped tomatoes
- 2 C. minced onions
- 6 jalapeno peppers, chopped
- 2 tsp. ground cumin
- 2 T. salt
- 2 T. sugar
- 1/2 C. white vinegar
- 1 tsp. minced garlic
- 1 (15 oz.) can tomato sauce
- 1/2 (6 oz.) can tomato paste
- 1/2 C. ketchup
- 1 C. water

In a large saucepan, combine chopped tomatoes, minced onions, chopped jalapeno peppers, ground cumin, salt, sugar, vinegar, minced garlic, tomato sauce, tomato paste, ketchup and water. Bring mixture to a slow boil over medium heat. Reduce heat and let sauce simmer at least 2 hours. Let mixture cool completely. Using a funnel, transfer sauce to a decorative sealable bottle. Cover bottle tightly and store in refrigerator.

Attach a gift tag with directions on how to serve sauce.

Gift Tag Directions:

Tinglin' Tongue Hot Sauce

Use Tinglin' Tongue Hot Sauce in recipes calling for hot sauce or serve with eggs, tacos, burritos, chicken, pork, fish or anything that needs a kick! Store in refrigerator.

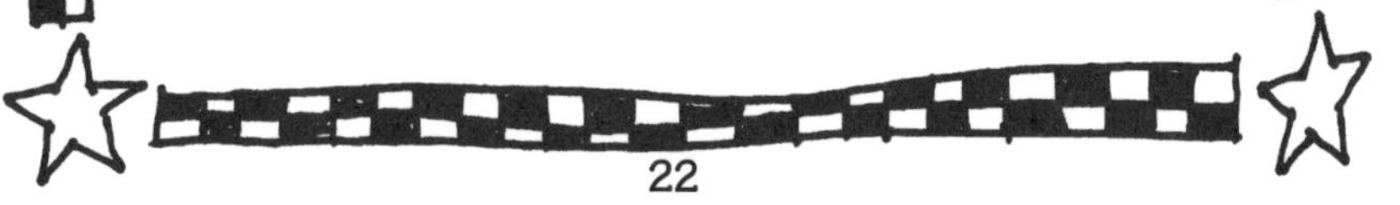

Tinglin' Tongue Hot Sauce

Use Tinglin' Tongue Hot Sauce in recipes calling for hot sauce or serve with eggs, tacos, burritos, chicken, pork, fish or anything that needs a kick! Store in refrigerator.

Tinglin' Tongue Hot Sauce

Use Tinglin' Tongue Hot Sauce in recipes calling for hot sauce or serve with eggs, tacos, burritos, chicken, pork, fish or anything that needs a kick! Store in refrigerator.

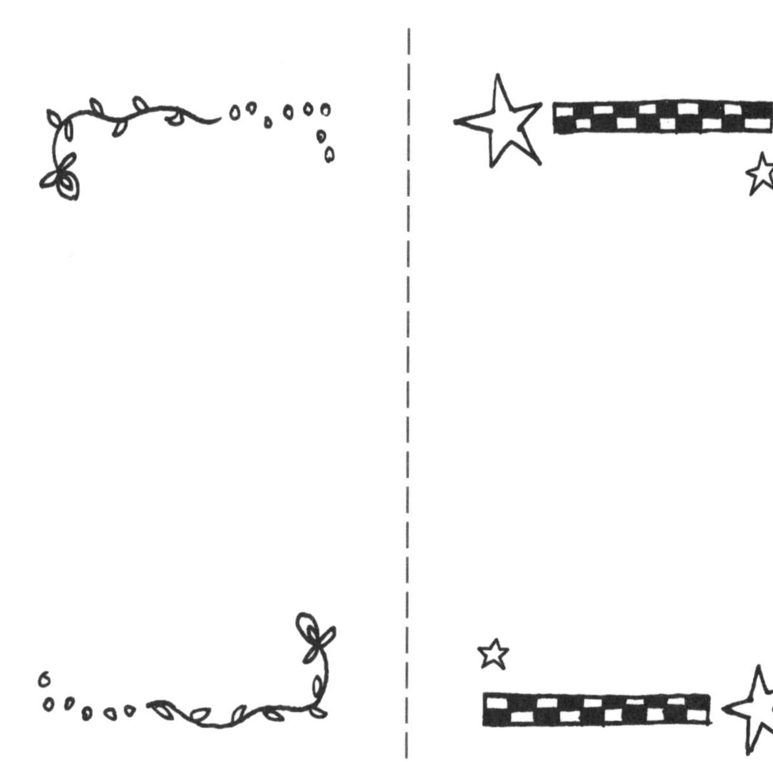

Tinglin' Tongue Hot Sauce

Use Tinglin' Tongue Hot Sauce in recipes calling for hot sauce or serve with eggs, tacos, burritos, chicken, pork, fish or anything that needs a kick! Store in refrigerator.

Tinglin' Tongue Hot Sauce

Use Tinglin' Tongue Hot Sauce in recipes calling for hot sauce or serve with eggs, tacos, burritos, chicken, pork, fish or anything that needs a kick! Store in refrigerator.

Teriyaki Sauce

Makes 2 1/2 cups

- 2 T. scallions, finely chopped
- 3 cloves garlic, minced
- 1 T. grated fresh ginger root
- 1 tsp. sesame oil
- 1 C. soy sauce
- 1/2 C. sherry cooking wine or Japanese sake
- 3 T. sugar
- 3/4 C. chicken broth
- 1 tsp. cornstarch

In a large saucepan over medium heat, cook chopped scallions, minced garlic and grated ginger root in sesame oil. Heat slowly for a few minutes. Add soy sauce, sherry or sake, sugar and chicken broth. Bring mixture to a boil. Reduce heat and let simmer for 10 minutes. In a small bowl, blend cornstarch with a little water. Add some of the hot liquid to the cornstarch mixture. Pour cornstarch mixture back into hot liquid in saucepan. Return liquid to a boil, stirring frequently. Reduce heat and let simmer until sauce thickens, about 2 to 3 minutes. Using a funnel, transfer sauce to a decorative sealable bottle. Cover bottle tightly and store in refrigerator up to 10 days.

Attach a gift tag with directions on how to serve sauce.

Gift Tag Directions:

Teriyaki Sauce

Use Teriyaki Sauce as a dipping sauce or marinade for chicken, beef or pork. Also good when brushed over skewered meat and vegetables. Store in refrigerator and discard after 10 days.

Teriyaki Sauce

Use Teriyaki Sauce as a dipping sauce or marinade for chicken, beef or pork. Also good when brushed over skewered meat and vegetables. Store in refrigerator and discard after 10 days.

Teriyaki Sauce

Use Teriyaki Sauce as a dipping sauce or marinade for chicken, beef or pork. Also good when brushed over skewered meat and vegetables. Store in refrigerator and discard after 10 days.

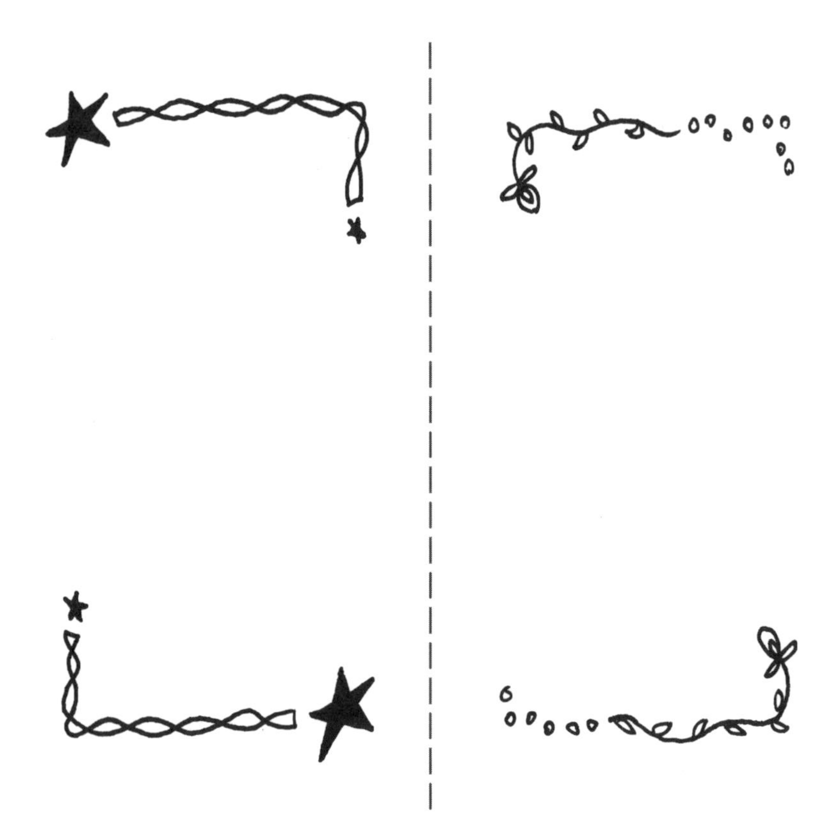

Teriyaki Sauce

Use Teriyaki Sauce as a dipping sauce or marinade for chicken, beef or pork. Also good when brushed over skewered meat and vegetables. Store in refrigerator and discard after 10 days.

Teriyaki Sauce

Use Teriyaki Sauce as a dipping sauce or marinade for chicken, beef or pork. Also good when brushed over skewered meat and vegetables. Store in refrigerator and discard after 10 days.

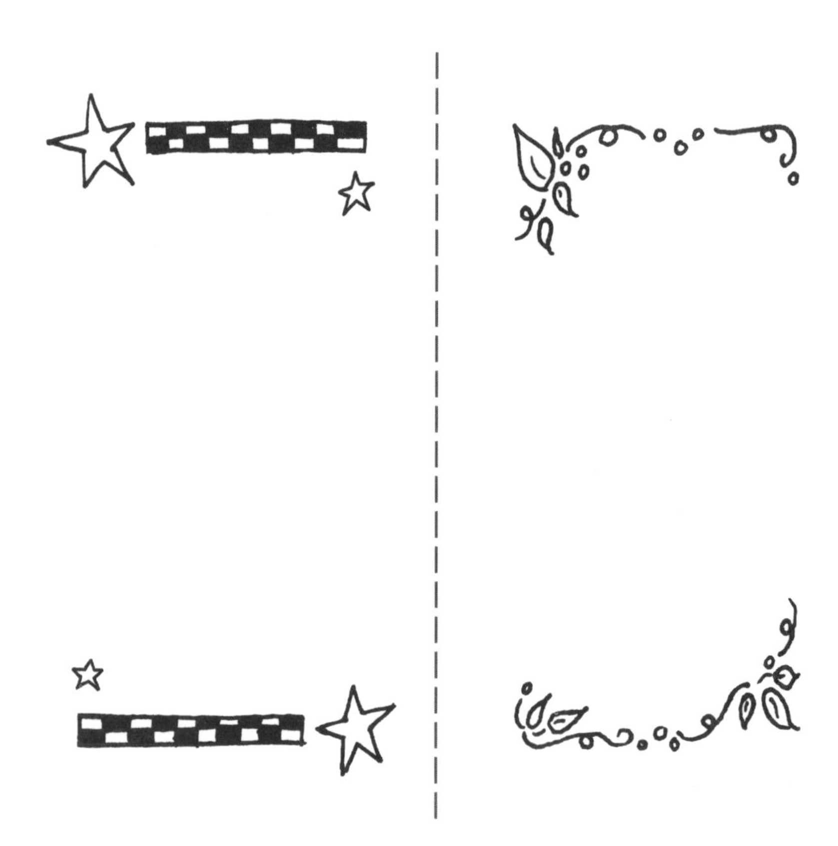

I Like it Hot, Hot, Hot Sauce

Makes 1 quart

1 onion, chopped
1 T. vegetable oil
2 cloves garlic, minced
1 C. carrots, chopped
2 C. water
3 Habanero peppers, minced
3 T. fresh lime juice
3 T. white vinegar
1 tsp. salt

In a large skillet, sauté onions in vegetable oil, until soft and transparent. Add minced garlic, chopped carrots and water. Bring mixture to a boil. Reduce heat and simmer until carrots are softened. Remove skillet from heat. Add minced Habanero peppers, lime juice, vinegar and salt. In a blender or food processor, puree mixture until smooth. Using a funnel, transfer sauce into a decorative sealable bottle. Cover bottle tightly and store in refrigerator.

Attach a gift tag with directions on how to serve sauce.

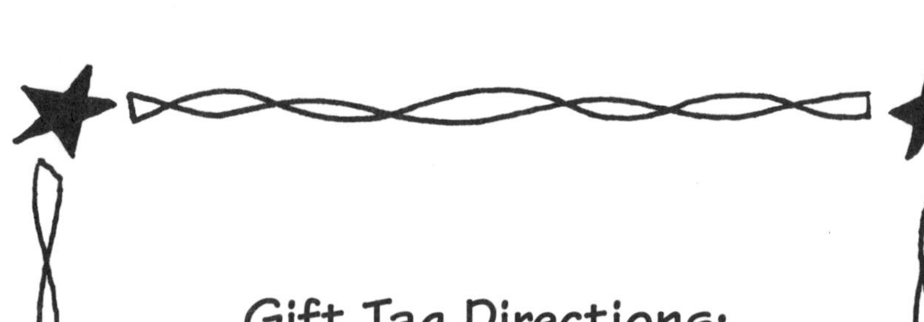

Gift Tag Directions:

I Like it Hot, Hot, Hot Sauce

Use I Like it Hot, Hot, Hot Sauce in recipes calling for hot sauce or serve with eggs, tacos, burritos, chicken, pork, fish or anything that needs a kick! Store in refrigerator.

I Like it Hot, Hot, Hot Sauce

Use I Like it Hot, Hot, Hot Sauce in recipes calling for hot sauce or serve with eggs, tacos, burritos, chicken, pork, fish or anything that needs a kick! Store in refrigerator.

I Like it Hot, Hot, Hot Sauce

Use I Like it Hot, Hot, Hot Sauce in recipes calling for hot sauce or serve with eggs, tacos, burritos, chicken, pork, fish or anything that needs a kick! Store in refrigerator.

I Like it Hot, Hot, Hot Sauce

Use I Like it Hot, Hot, Hot Sauce in recipes calling for hot sauce or serve with eggs, tacos, burritos, chicken, pork, fish or anything that needs a kick! Store in refrigerator.

I Like it Hot, Hot, Hot Sauce

Use I Like it Hot, Hot, Hot Sauce in recipes calling for hot sauce or serve with eggs, tacos, burritos, chicken, pork, fish or anything that needs a kick! Store in refrigerator.

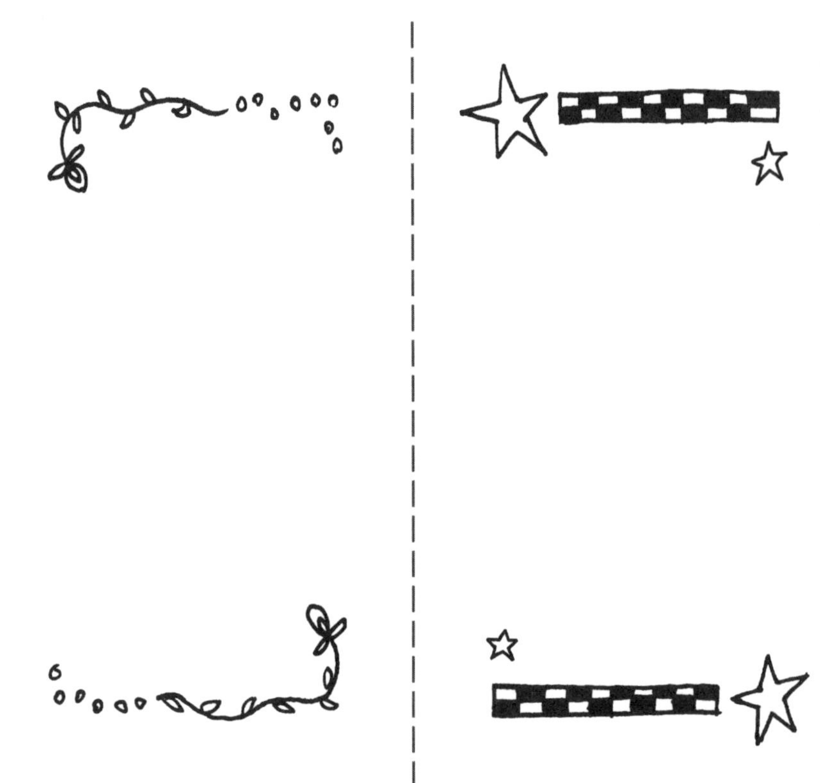

Blue Ribbon BBQ Sauce

Makes 2 1/2 cups

1 C. ketchup
1 T. Worcestershire sauce
1 C. molasses
2 T. brown sugar
1/4 C. chopped onions
1 T. garlic powder
3/4 tsp. pepper
1/2 tsp. cayenne pepper
2 T. lemon juice
1 (5 1/2 oz.) can tomato juice
2 T. liquid smoke flavoring

In a blender or food processor, combine ketchup, Worcestershire sauce, molasses, brown sugar, chopped onions, garlic powder, pepper, cayenne pepper, lemon juice, tomato juice and liquid smoke flavoring. Puree mixture until smooth. Transfer mixture to a small saucepan over medium heat. Bring to a boil then reduce heat to low. Let simmer for approximately 1 hour, until sauce reaches desired thickness. Using a funnel, transfer sauce to a decorative sealable bottle. Cover bottle tightly and store in refrigerator.

Attach a gift tag with directions on how to serve sauce.

Gift Tag Directions:

Blue Ribbon BBQ Sauce

Use Blue Ribbon BBQ Sauce as a dipping sauce for meat, smothered over steaks, pork or chicken or in recipes calling for barbeque sauce. Store in refrigerator.

Blue Ribbon BBQ Sauce

Use Blue Ribbon BBQ Sauce as a dipping sauce for meat, smothered over steaks, pork or chicken or in recipes calling for barbeque sauce. Store in refrigerator.

Blue Ribbon BBQ Sauce

Use Blue Ribbon BBQ Sauce as a dipping sauce for meat, smothered over steaks, pork or chicken or in recipes calling for barbeque sauce. Store in refrigerator.

Blue Ribbon BBQ Sauce

Use Blue Ribbon BBQ Sauce as a dipping sauce for meat, smothered over steaks, pork or chicken or in recipes calling for barbeque sauce. Store in refrigerator.

Blue Ribbon BBQ Sauce

Use Blue Ribbon BBQ Sauce as a dipping sauce for meat, smothered over steaks, pork or chicken or in recipes calling for barbeque sauce. Store in refrigerator.

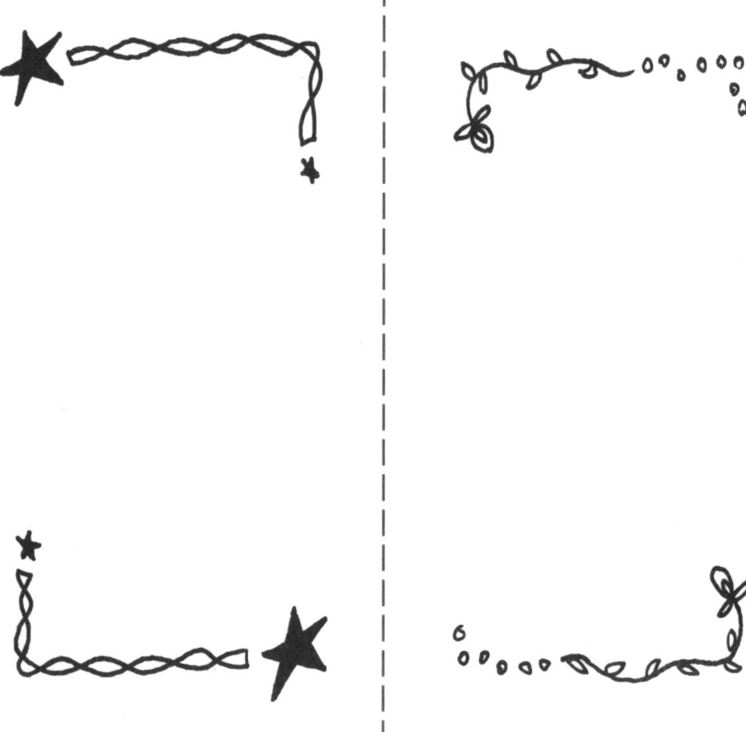

Caramel Bourbon Vanilla Sauce

Makes 3 1/2 cups

2 C. sugar
1/2 C. water
1 C. heavy cream
1 vanilla bean, split in half lengthwise
2 tsp. lemon juice
2 T. unsalted butter
1 T. bourbon whiskey

In a 2-quart saucepan over medium heat, combine sugar and water. Without stirring, cook mixture until darkened in color. Cook about 20 minutes, carefully swirling the pan a few times. Reduce to low heat and slowly add heavy cream, stirring with a wooden spoon. Using a knife, scrape vanilla seeds from pod. Add vanilla seeds and pod to pan. Add lemon juice, butter and bourbon whiskey. Stir until well combined. Using a funnel, transfer sauce to a decorative sealable bottle. Cover bottle tightly and store in refrigerator up to 1 week.

Attach a gift tag with directions on how to serve sauce.

Gift Tag Directions:

Caramel Bourbon Vanilla Sauce

Microwave Caramel Bourbon Vanilla Sauce in 15 second periods until sauce reaches desired pouring consistency. Use sauce as a topping for ice cream or drizzled over chocolate brownies. Store in refrigerator and discard after 1 week.

Caramel Bourbon Vanilla Sauce

Microwave Caramel Bourbon Vanilla Sauce in 15 second periods until sauce reaches desired pouring consistency. Use sauce as a topping for ice cream or drizzled over chocolate brownies. Store in refrigerator and discard after 1 week.

Caramel Bourbon Vanilla Sauce

Microwave Caramel Bourbon Vanilla Sauce in 15 second periods until sauce reaches desired pouring consistency. Use sauce as a topping for ice cream or drizzled over chocolate brownies. Store in refrigerator and discard after 1 week.

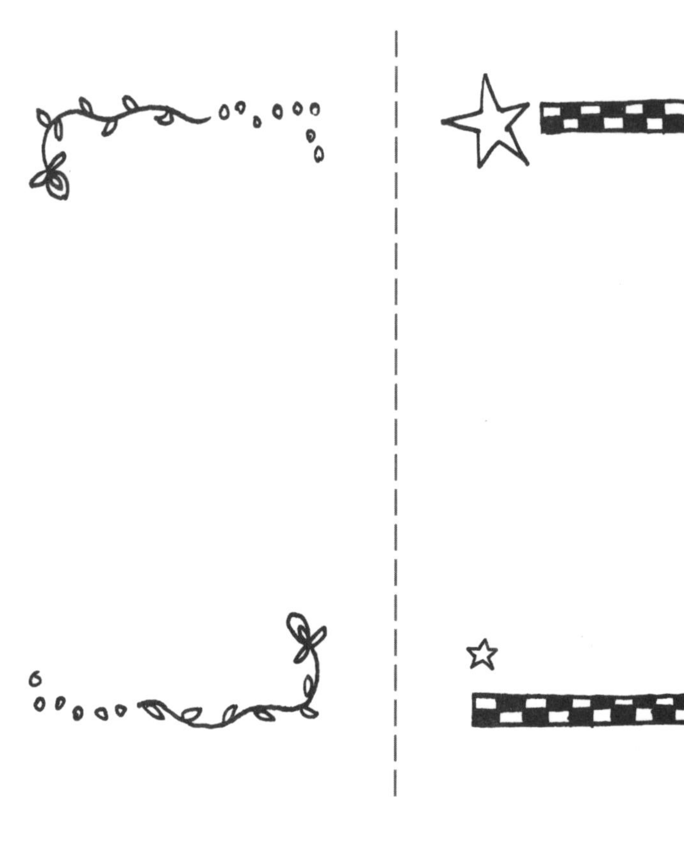

Caramel Bourbon Vanilla Sauce

Microwave Caramel Bourbon Vanilla Sauce in 15 second periods until sauce reaches desired pouring consistency. Use sauce as a topping for ice cream or drizzled over chocolate brownies. Store in refrigerator and discard after 1 week.

Caramel Bourbon Vanilla Sauce

Microwave Caramel Bourbon Vanilla Sauce in 15 second periods until sauce reaches desired pouring consistency. Use sauce as a topping for ice cream or drizzled over chocolate brownies. Store in refrigerator and discard after 1 week.

Liquid Fire Hot Sauce

Makes 1 quart

12 Habanero peppers, diced
1 (15 1/2 oz.) can sliced peaches in juice
1/2 C. dark molasses
1/2 C. yellow mustard
1/2 C. brown sugar
1 C. white vinegar
2 T. salt
2 T. paprika
1 T. pepper
1 T. cumin
1/2 tsp. coriander
1/2 tsp. ground ginger
1/2 tsp. allspice

In a blender or food processor, combine diced Habanero peppers, sliced peaches in juice, molasses, mustard, brown sugar and vinegar. Add salt, paprika, pepper, cumin, coriander, ginger and allspice. Blend until liquefied. Using a funnel, transfer sauce to a decorative sealable bottle. Cover bottle tightly and store in refrigerator.

Attach a gift tag with directions on how to serve sauce.

Gift Tag Directions:

Liquid Fire Hot Sauce

Use Liquid Fire Hot Sauce in recipes calling for hot sauce or serve with eggs, steak, tacos, burritos, pizza or anything that needs a kick! Store in refrigerator.

Liquid Fire
Hot Sauce

Use Liquid Fire Hot Sauce in recipes calling for hot sauce or serve with eggs, steak, tacos, burritos, pizza or anything that needs a kick! Store in refrigerator.

Liquid Fire
Hot Sauce

Use Liquid Fire Hot Sauce in recipes calling for hot sauce or serve with eggs, steak, tacos, burritos, pizza or anything that needs a kick! Store in refrigerator.

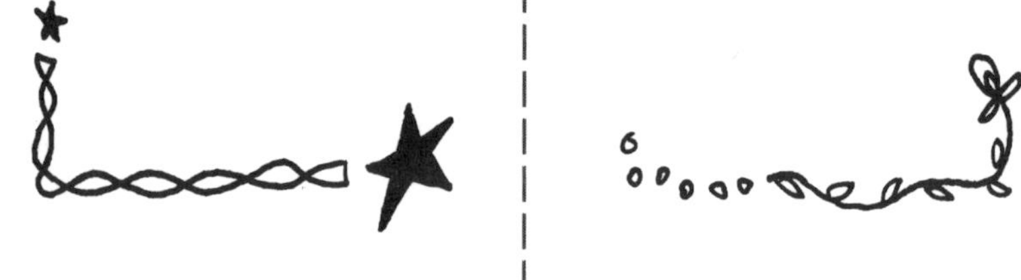

Liquid Fire Hot Sauce

Use Liquid Fire Hot Sauce in recipes calling for hot sauce or serve with eggs, steak, tacos, burritos, pizza or anything that needs a kick! Store in refrigerator.

Liquid Fire Hot Sauce

Use Liquid Fire Hot Sauce in recipes calling for hot sauce or serve with eggs, steak, tacos, burritos, pizza or anything that needs a kick! Store in refrigerator.

Tequila Cocktail Sauce

Makes 2 1/4 cups

3/4 C. ketchup
3/4 C. chili sauce
1/4 C. prepared horseradish
2 T. Worcestershire sauce
1 T. plus 1 1/2 tsp. lemon juice
1 1/2 tsp. hot pepper sauce
1/4 C. tequila
Salt and pepper to taste

In a large bowl, combine ketchup, chili sauce, horseradish, Worcestershire sauce, lemon juice, hot pepper sauce, tequila, salt and pepper. Mix until well blended. Using a funnel, transfer sauce to a decorative sealable bottle. Cover bottle tightly and store in refrigerator.

Attach a gift tag with directions on how to serve sauce.

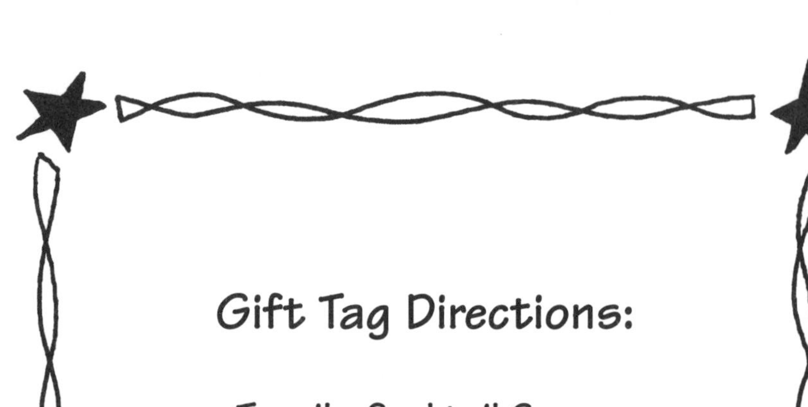

Gift Tag Directions:

Tequila Cocktail Sauce

Use Tequila Cocktail Sauce as a dipping sauce for shrimp or crabmeat or use in recipes calling for cocktail sauce. Store in refrigerator.

Tequila Cocktail Sauce

Use Tequila Cocktail Sauce as a dipping sauce for shrimp or crabmeat or use in recipes calling for cocktail sauce. Store in refrigerator.

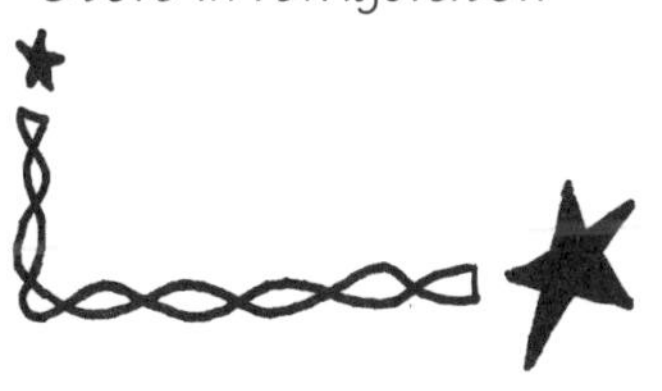

Tequila Cocktail Sauce

Use Tequila Cocktail Sauce as a dipping sauce for shrimp or crabmeat or use in recipes calling for cocktail sauce. Store in refrigerator.

Tequila Cocktail Sauce

Use Tequila Cocktail Sauce as a dipping sauce for shrimp or crabmeat or use in recipes calling for cocktail sauce. Store in refrigerator.

Tequila Cocktail Sauce

Use Tequila Cocktail Sauce as a dipping sauce for shrimp or crabmeat or use in recipes calling for cocktail sauce. Store in refrigerator.

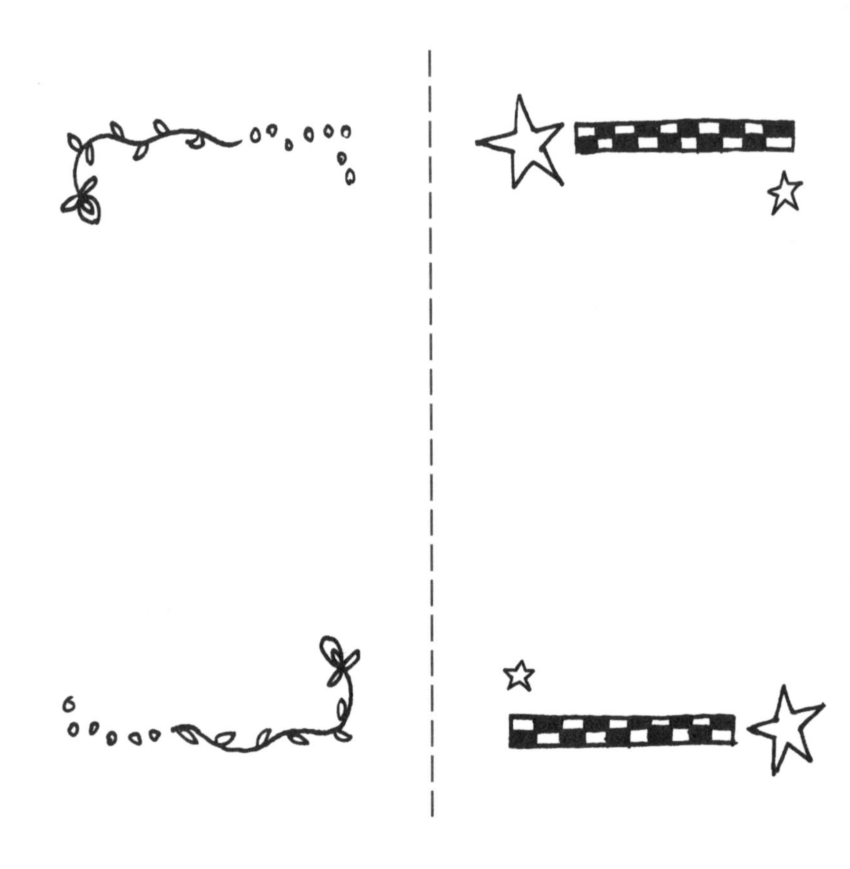

Honey Mustard Dipping Sauce

Makes 1 cup

1/2 C. mayonnaise
2 T. prepared mustard
2 T. honey
1 T. lemon juice

In a small bowl, whisk together mayonnaise, mustard, honey and lemon juice until well blended. Place in a decorative sealable bottle. Cover bottle tightly and store in refrigerator up to 10 days.

Attach a gift tag with directions on how to serve sauce.

Gift Tag Directions:

Honey Mustard Dipping Sauce

Use Honey Mustard Dipping Sauce as a dipping sauce for chicken tenders or French fries. Also good poured over baked or grilled chicken. Store in refrigerator and discard after 10 days.

Honey Mustard Dipping Sauce

Use Honey Mustard Dipping Sauce as a dipping sauce for chicken tenders or French fries. Also good poured over baked or grilled chicken. Store in refrigerator and discard after 10 days.

Honey Mustard Dipping Sauce

Use Honey Mustard Dipping Sauce as a dipping sauce for chicken tenders or French fries. Also good poured over baked or grilled chicken. Store in refrigerator and discard after 10 days.

Honey Mustard Dipping Sauce

Use Honey Mustard Dipping Sauce as a dipping sauce for chicken tenders or French fries. Also good poured over baked or grilled chicken. Store in refrigerator and discard after 10 days.

Honey Mustard Dipping Sauce

Use Honey Mustard Dipping Sauce as a dipping sauce for chicken tenders or French fries. Also good poured over baked or grilled chicken. Store in refrigerator and discard after 10 days.

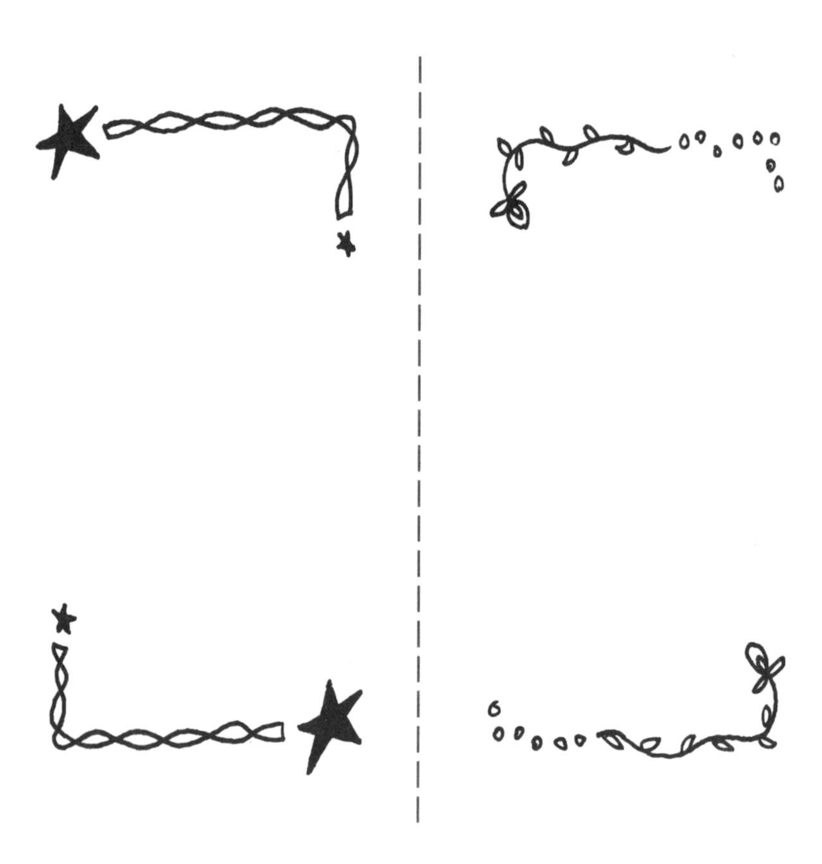

Vanilla Maple Syrup

Makes 1 quart

2 C. brown sugar
2 1/2 C. sugar
1/2 C. corn syrup, optional
1/4 tsp. salt
2 C. water
1/2 tsp. vanilla
1/2 tsp. maple extract

In a large saucepan, mix brown sugar, sugar, corn syrup, salt and water. Bring mixture to a boil. Boil for 3 minutes, 5 minutes if not using corn syrup, without stirring. Add vanilla and maple extract. Using a funnel, transfer syrup to a decorative sealable bottle. Cover bottle tightly and store in refrigerator.

Attach a gift tag with directions on how to serve syrup.

Gift Tag Directions:

Vanilla Maple Syrup

Heat Vanilla Maple Syrup in microwave for 1 to 1 1/2 minutes. Use syrup as a topping for pancakes or waffles.

Vanilla Maple Syrup

Heat Vanilla Maple Syrup in microwave for 1 to 1 1/2 minutes. Use syrup as a topping for pancakes or waffles.

Vanilla Maple Syrup

Heat Vanilla Maple Syrup in microwave for 1 to 1 1/2 minutes. Use syrup as a topping for pancakes or waffles.

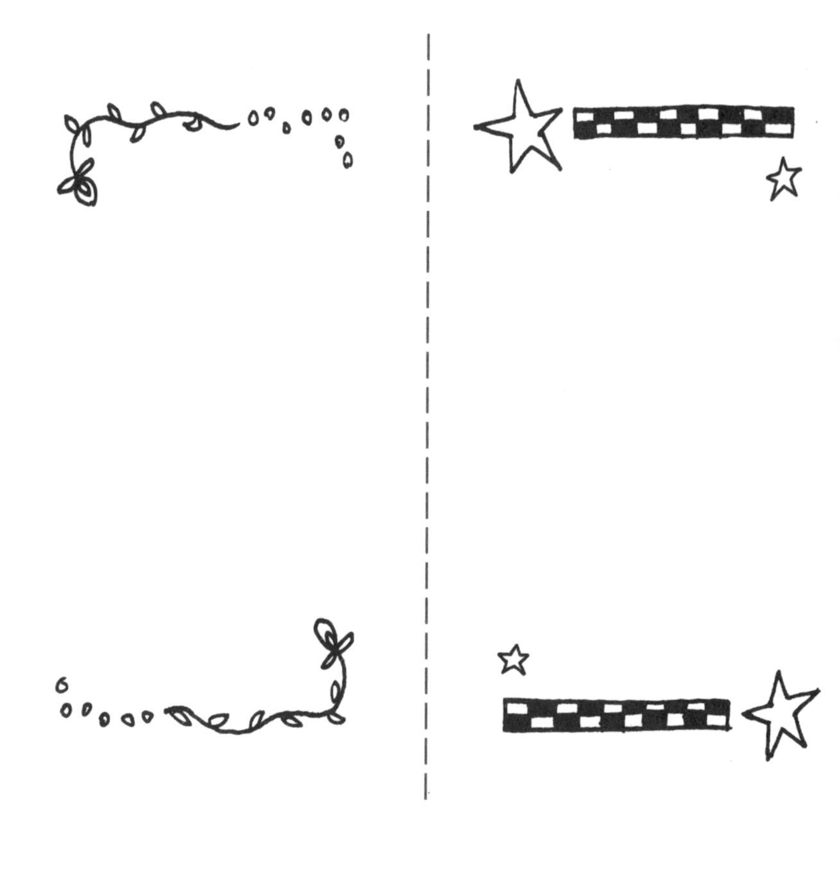

Vanilla Maple Syrup

Heat Vanilla Maple Syrup in microwave for 1 to 1 1/2 minutes. Use syrup as a topping for pancakes or waffles.

Vanilla Maple Syrup

Heat Vanilla Maple Syrup in microwave for 1 to 1 1/2 minutes. Use syrup as a topping for pancakes or waffles.

Mango Hot Sauce

Makes 1 1/2 quarts

4 Habanero peppers, seeded
1/2 tsp. salt
2 C. water
3 mangos, peeled and seeded
3 kiwis, peeled
Juice of 2 limes
Juice of 1 1/2 lemons
2 T. frozen orange juice concentrate
2 T. white vinegar

In a large pot, combine diced and seeded Habanero peppers, salt and water. Bring to a boil over medium heat. Reduce heat and let simmer for 15 minutes. Drain pot, reserving 3/4 cup water. In a blender or food processor, puree drained Habanero peppers, peeled mangos, peeled kiwis, lime juice, lemon juice, orange juice concentrate and 3/4 cup reserved water. Return puree to pot and simmer, stirring constantly, over medium heat for 10 minutes. Remove from heat and add vinegar, stirring until slightly cooled. Using a funnel, transfer sauce to a decorative sealable bottle. Cover bottle tightly and store in refrigerator.

Attach a gift tag with directions on how to serve sauce.

Gift Tag Directions:

Mango Hot Sauce

Use Mango Hot Sauce in recipes calling for hot sauce or serve with chicken, pork, fish or anything that needs a kick! Store in refrigerator.

Mango Hot Sauce

Use Mango Hot Sauce in recipes calling for hot sauce or serve with chicken, pork, fish or anything that needs a kick! Store in refrigerator.

Mango Hot Sauce

Use Mango Hot Sauce in recipes calling for hot sauce or serve with chicken, pork, fish or anything that needs a kick! Store in refrigerator.

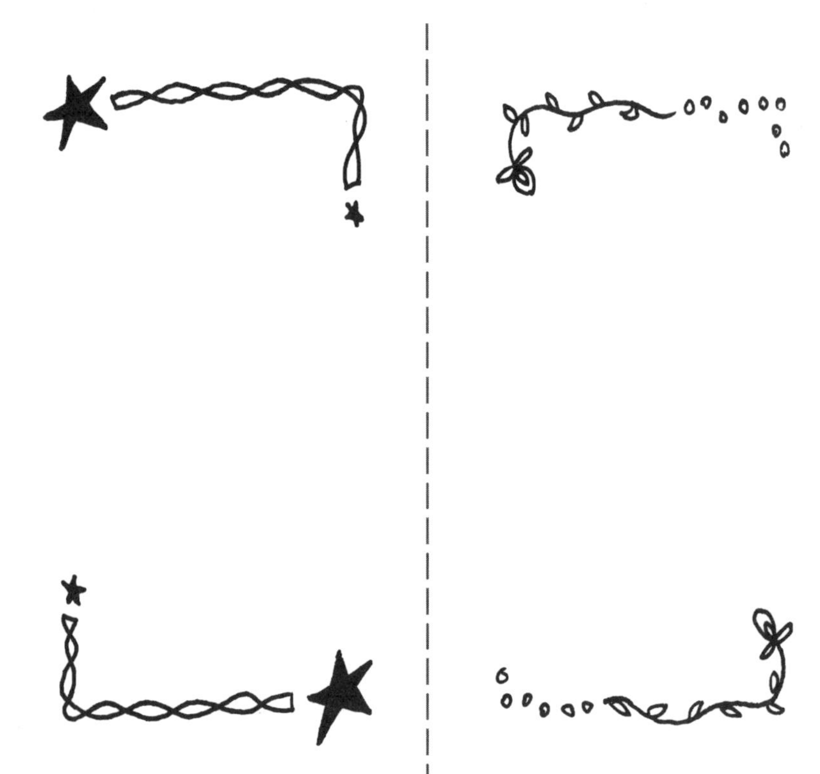

Mango Hot Sauce

Use Mango Hot Sauce in recipes calling for hot sauce or serve with chicken, pork, fish or anything that needs a kick! Store in refrigerator.

Mango Hot Sauce

Use Mango Hot Sauce in recipes calling for hot sauce or serve with chicken, pork, fish or anything that needs a kick! Store in refrigerator.

Bourbon Whiskey BBQ Sauce

Makes 1 quart

- 1/2 onion, chopped
- 4 cloves garlic, minced
- 3/4 C. bourbon whiskey
- 1/2 tsp. pepper
- 1/2 T. salt
- 2 C. ketchup
- 1/4 C. tomato paste
- 1/3 C. cider vinegar
- 2 T. liquid smoke flavoring
- 1/4 C. Worcestershire sauce
- 1/2 C. brown sugar
- 1/2 tsp. hot pepper sauce

In a large skillet, combine chopped onions, minced garlic and bourbon whiskey over medium heat. Sauté for 10 minutes, until onions are transparent. Add pepper, salt, ketchup, tomato paste, vinegar, liquid smoke flavoring, Worcestershire sauce, brown sugar and hot pepper sauce. Mix until well blended and bring to a boil. Reduce heat to low medium and let simmer for 20 minutes. If smooth sauce is preferred, transfer to a blender or food processor and puree. Using a funnel, transfer sauce to a decorative sealable bottle. Cover bottle tightly and store in refrigerator.

Attach a gift tag with directions on how to serve sauce.

Gift Tag Directions:

Bourbon Whiskey BBQ Sauce

Use Bourbon Whiskey BBQ Sauce as a dipping sauce for meat, smothered over steaks, pork or chicken or in recipes calling for barbeque sauce. Store in refrigerator.

Bourbon Whiskey BBQ Sauce

Use Bourbon Whiskey BBQ Sauce as a dipping sauce for meat, smothered over steaks, pork or chicken or in recipes calling for barbeque sauce. Store in refrigerator.

Bourbon Whiskey BBQ Sauce

Use Bourbon Whiskey BBQ Sauce as a dipping sauce for meat, smothered over steaks, pork or chicken or in recipes calling for barbeque sauce. Store in refrigerator.

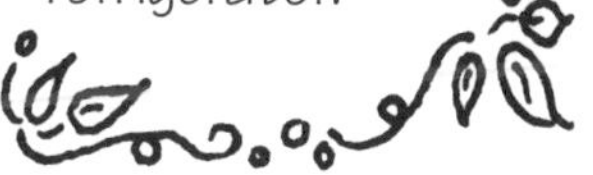

Bourbon Whiskey BBQ Sauce

Use Bourbon Whiskey BBQ Sauce as a dipping sauce for meat, smothered over steaks, pork or chicken or in recipes calling for barbeque sauce. Store in refrigerator.

Bourbon Whiskey BBQ Sauce

Use Bourbon Whiskey BBQ Sauce as a dipping sauce for meat, smothered over steaks, pork or chicken or in recipes calling for barbeque sauce. Store in refrigerator.

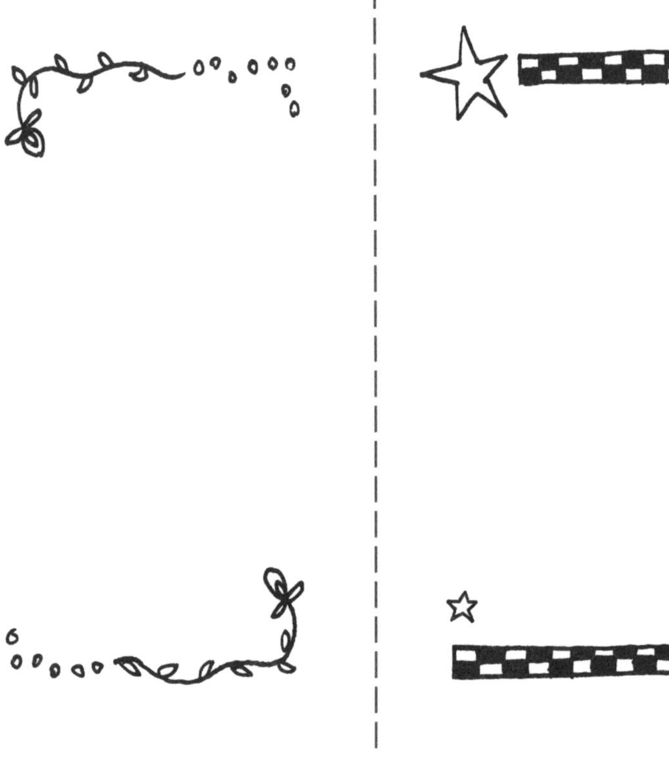

Index

Recipes Shown on Front Cover

From left to right

See our entire line!
Visit www.cqproducts.com
or call 866*804*9892
for a catalog
Gifts in a Jar
Holiday Fun
Gifts in a Bottle
Liqueurs
Gifts in a Jar
Cocoas Cappuccinos Coffees & Teas
Gifts in a Bag
1 Master Mix
51 Muffins

To purchase more books by
CQ Products
see your local gift or craft store!
Or call to order a FREE catalog at 866-804-9892
CQ Products
507 Industrial St.
Waverly, IA 50677
www.cqproducts.com • fax 800-886-7496